"Ironically, many P
with Baptist convicti
of infant baptism on the grounds that, at least in their opinion,
the Bible, or, primarily the *New Testament*, is silent regarding
the practice. Yet, there is something about the Reformed theology of infant baptism that they desperately want to believe.
Thus, the practice of public child dedication has become part
of their tradition as a replacement. Brian Najapfour has presented a straightforward and helpful analysis of the practice
of child dedication with pointed marks of contrast with covenant baptism. He concurs with the notion that Christian
parents should dedicate and consecrate their children to the
Lord in thanksgiving for them as God's gift. But, Najapfour
demonstrates convincingly that there is no biblical warrant for
transforming a private commitment into a public ceremony
and thus integrating it into a public worship service. I certainly
recommend Najapfour's booklet to those who may be wrestling with the issue. It is a fair, concise, and biblical treatment."

—Dr. Michael Barrett, Academic Dean and Professor
of Old Testament, Puritan Reformed Theological Seminary

"Though readers may not agree with every conclusion that
Najapfour makes, he provides a helpful historical survey and
thoughtful biblical reflection on the practice of child dedication. I commend this book to you."

—Dr. Robert L. Plummer, Professor of New Testament
Interpretation, The Southern Baptist Theological Seminary

"In this brief booklet, Brian Najapfour has written about a
matter that is getting a lot of attention in some circles. Some of
those who hold to believers' baptism have adopted a practice

of child dedication. Out of concern for their infants, they feel a need to dedicate their children to the Lord in a formal way. Perhaps they regard this as an alternative to infant baptism—but is it? Najapfour does not think so. Although he commends his Baptist friends for showing their love and concern for the children God has entrusted to their care, Najapfour convincingly argues that the practice of child dedication cannot be defended on biblical grounds. Nowhere in the Bible do we read that God requires this ceremony of His people."

"Dedicating our children to the Lord is a good thing, but care must be taken lest too much emphasis is placed on the action of parents rather than on God's action towards our children. It is our gracious God who takes believing parents and their children into His covenant and church. This booklet serves as a much needed reminder of this glorious fact."

—Rev. Cornelis (Niel) Pronk, Emeritus Pastor of
Free Reformed Church, Brantford, Ontario

"Many Christian churches 'dedicate' the children of believers. They do this because they believe there is something different about these children in contrast to the children of the world and because they believe Christian parents have holy duties towards their children. What most churches and parents do not realize is that by engaging in this practice they are doing so for the same reasons Reformed churches *baptize* their children. If you are wrestling with whether to dedicate or baptize your child, I commend Brian Najapfour's little book to you. It will lead you in what Scripture teaches and lead you in raising your children in the fear and instruction of the Lord."

—Rev. Daniel R. Hyde, Pastor, Oceanside United Reformed Church,
Oceanside, California; author, *God in Our Midst*;
Welcome to a Reformed Church; and *Why Believe in God?*

CHILD DEDICATION

Considered Historically, Theologically, and Pastorally

Brian G. Najapfour

BIBLICAL SPIRITUALITY PRESS

Child Dedication: Considered Historically, Theologically, and Pastorally

Published by

Biblical Spirituality Press
6940 Hanna Lake Ave., SE
Caledonia, MI 49316
Phone (616) 698-7467
E-mail: biblicalspiritualitypress@gmail.com
Website: biblicalspiritualitypress.org

ISBN: 978-0-9889498-1-2

Printed in the United States of America

To
Dr. Joel R. Beeke

my dear brother in Christ,
fellow laborer in the gospel,
and wise mentor in the ministry.

TABLE OF CONTENTS

FOREWORD

I welcome the opportunity to commend Rev. Brian Najap-four's study of the neglected subject but widespread practice of child dedication.

In a climate in which liberal or liberal-tending theologians utilize Scripture, in one way or another, as an exemplar of how to do theology rather than as a dictum of what our theology ought to be, we conservative Christians have upheld Scripture as our theological dictum but can be guilty of undercutting this stance by the acontextual and selective manner of its application. In short, our high *view* of Scripture is not always accompanied by a high *use* of it.

In illustrating this disjunction from the practice of child dedication, Brian Najapfour presents in a friendly and balanced fashion a corrective to the Baptist background from which he has come. Although he does not rule out absolutely the practice of child dedication, he injects certain considerations into the contemplation of its practice:

- The regulative principle of worship, by which we understand that only those elements instituted or appointed by command or example, or deduced from Scripture by good and necessary consequence, are permissible in worship, and that whatever is neither commanded nor deduced from Scripture is prohibited.

- The command to apply to the children of believers the sign of the covenant essential to the richer meaning of baptism.

- The absence of the command to practice child dedication in the passages cited in support of it.

- The notion of the parents' dedication of their children to God inherent in infant baptism.

Understandably, those new to these considerations may balk initially.

As a conversation starter, Brian Najapfour successfully challenges, in my view, the thinking that child dedication is required by Scripture. He also raises the question, legitimately so, as to why some opposed to infant baptism desire a ceremony in worship tantamount in appearance to an infant baptism without the water (*i.e.*, the sign of the covenant). I suspect in the longer run, however, that the widespread return to the sacrament of infant baptism will require either more researching of Scripture by those currently unconvinced of the sacrament as applied to children, or a more balanced approach by its advocates in which the responsibilities of covenant children are stressed as much as their privileges.

Without further ado, let the conversation begin!

—Dr. Tim J.R. Trumper
Senior Minister, Seventh Reformed Church
Grand Rapids, Michigan (www.7thref.org)

ACKNOWLEDGMENTS

I would like to thank Ryan Hurd, Anna Renkema, and Gina Bessetti-Reyes for their editing expertise. Ryan, I especially thank you for reading and re-reading the manuscript to improve the clarity of this booklet. I am also grateful to Gary den Hollander for his proofreading help, to Linda den Hollander for her pleasant typesetting, and to Amy Zevenbergen for the creative cover design.

A special word of gratitude also goes to my dear wife Sarah for her unceasing encouragement.

And last but not the least, I thank and praise God for giving me the right to become His child through faith in His Son Jesus Christ (John 1:12).

INTRODUCTION

I grew up in a Baptist church that practices child dedication. Remember, however, that not all Baptist churches
hold to this practice, as some churches do not permit such
a custom at all.[1] With this fact in mind, whenever I refer
to Baptists in this booklet, I mean Baptists who argue for a
child dedication service. As support for this type of dedicatory service, Baptists use the example of Hannah's bringing
her son Samuel to the house of the Lord (1 Sam. 1:24) and
the example of Mary and Joseph's bringing the infant Jesus
to the temple (Luke 2:22). With careful analysis of these
passages, this study will consider whether child dedication
is biblically mandated and therefore required. Towards an
understanding of the issue, prior to surveying the biblical
data, I will first define child dedication as understood by its
proponents and second trace its historical origin. The study
will close with some pastoral notes and suggestions helpful
for those who struggle with the issue.

---

1. For a critique of child dedication service from a Calvinistic Baptist
perspective, see Richard Barcellos, *Baby Dedications Ancient and Modern:
Are They Biblical?* (Fullerton: Reformed Baptist Publication, n. d.).

CHAPTER 1

DEFINING CHILD DEDICATION

Child dedication, otherwise called infant or baby dedication, is generally understood by its Baptist supporters as a solemn church service in which Christian parents publicly present a newborn child to the Lord.[1] This basic definition of child dedication indicates that only believing parents can present their child to God. Unbelieving parents must first surrender their lives to God by faith in the Lord Jesus Christ before they can present their child to the living God. Since "without faith *it is* impossible to please [God]" (Heb. 11:6),[2] God will by no means take pleasure in the act of the unbelievers in the presentation of their child.

Perhaps one may ask, "If child dedication is only for Christian parents, and only *one* of the parents is a believer, will the dedication service still be pleasing to God?" In

---

1. Others call this rite "family dedication, child presentation, blessing of children, or a service of thanksgiving and covenant." See Richard C. Leonard, "Child Dedication," in *The Sacred Actions of Christian Worship*, ed. Robert E. Webber (Nashville: Star Song Publishing Group, 1994), 267.

2. In this paper quotations from the Bible are taken from the New King James Version.

this case, Baptists still maintain the principle of the Bible: "without faith *it is* impossible to please [God]." Therefore, for an unbelieving parent, the act of dedicating will not bring pleasure to God.

One may ask an additional question, "Does God take pleasure in the dedication of a child, since no one, except God, knows if that child is elect?" To answer this question, Baptists would argue that, in a dedication service, the child is totally passive. Thus, baby dedication may also be called "parent dedication"[3] to emphasize the activity of parents towards God. Child dedication is not the act of the child's committing himself to God, but the act of the parents' committing their child to God. Neither is child dedication viewed as God making a covenant with parents for their child. Rather, it is the parents that are making a covenant with God to rear their child in the fear of the Lord.

Noticeably, both child dedication and infant baptism carry the concept of covenant. The former emphasizes the parents' covenant with God for their child (human promise). The latter, in contrast, emphasizes God's covenant with the parents for their child (divine promise). That is, a divine promise that if their child will also believe in Jesus Christ, God will save their child. From a paedobaptistic point of view, the difference between the two is aptly put by Daniel R. Hyde:

---

3. Marion D. Aldrige, "The Parent-Child Dedication Service," in *The Pastors' Guide Book: A Manual for Worship* (Nashville: Broadman Press, 1984), 121.

"Dedication" services…focus attention on the action of the parents. Infant baptism, on the other hand, focuses our attention and our hearts upon God's action, which we receive through faith alone…. Whereas dedication looks back and says, "We gave you to the Lord," baptism looks back and says, "The Lord gave himself to you in the promise of washing away your sins."[4]

For Baptists, the basic purpose of child dedication is simply to present a child to God publicly. This presentation is accompanied with a recognition from the parents that their child is a blessing from God and that they are now making a vow to Him, by His grace, to foster their child in the Christian faith. The Neighborhood Church of Castro Valley explains: "We view infant dedication as an act in which parents honor God publicly through acknowledging (1) that their child is a gift from God and (2) that they are committed as parents to partner with God in fulfilling His purposes for their child."[5]

Members of the congregation are also involved in child dedication, for they are expected to help the parents fulfill their pledge to God. As Mahan Siler, a Baptist pastor, states:

The congregation is also involved in covenant making. The church family is forever different for having

4. Daniel R. Hyde, *Jesus Loves the Little Children: Why We Baptize Children* (Grandville: Reformed Fellowship, Inc., 2006), 53.

5. Neighborhood Church of Castro Valley, CA, "Infant Dedication Services"; accessed 9 November 2011; available from http://www.3crosses.org/neighborhood/pages/7-infant-dedication-services; Internet.

children joining its life together. While not yet respon-
sible, baptized members, these infants are nevertheless
incorporated into the family of faith. The parents
intentionally are placing their children into the sphere
of the church's influence, requesting in return the community for joint parenting.[6]

The above quote should resonate with paedobaptists
because of the communal concept connected to it: namely,
that through the dedication service a child is "incorporated into the family of faith." Richard Leonard remarks,
"Theologically and in other ways…[child dedication] par-
allels infant baptism as a ceremony marking the child's
entrance into the Christian community and the beginning
of his or her journey along the path of Christian nurture
and training."[7] For Baptists, a child is incorporated into the
congregation of faith in the sense that, while not yet a baptized member, he is now physically part of a local church
where the child's parents are both physically and spiritu-
ally members (assuming that both are Christians and
members of that church).[8] The paedobaptists, in contrast,
believe that a child of believing parents can be a member
of a local church and that his membership is signified by

6. M. Mahan Siler, "Rites of Passage: A Meeting of Worship and Pastoral Care," *Review and Expositor* 85 (1988): 53.

7. Leonard, "Child Dedication," 268.

8. Some churches, such as the Neighbourhood Church of Castro Valley, think that "[p]arents do not have to be members of [a local church]
to dedicate their infants." See Neighborhood Church of Castro Valley, CA,
"Infant Dedication Services."

his baptism. However, paedobaptists do make a distinction between baptized members and confessing members, that is, those who have made a public profession of their faith in Christ. Since an infant has no capacity yet to comprehend the gospel, he cannot consciously confess Christ and therefore cannot be a confessing member. Yet, the baptized child is still counted as a member of a congregation.

Returning to the Baptists' view of the congregation's involvement, the congregation is expected to support the parents primarily in the spiritual development of the child being dedicated. This idea is well attested by the Baptist State Convention of North Carolina:

> The purpose of the parent/child dedication service is to publicly affirm *both the role of the parents and the congregation* in the spiritual nurture of the child being presented. While the child is presented for dedication, it is actually the parents *and the congregation* who actively enter into a covenant for the benefit of the child. A covenant is a solemn promise and should never be entered into lightly.
>
> During this service, the parents commit to raising their children according to scriptural mandates that place the responsibility for the spiritual nurture with the parents. The parents promise to impart Christian faith and principles and to live as examples of that faith. *The congregation, as their community of faith, covenants to support the parents and child in this pilgrimage and to also exemplify faith in their daily lives.*

Again, the responsibilities arising from a parent/
child dedication service fall *primarily with the parents
and secondarily with the congregation of faith.*[9]

To summarize our discussion on the definition of child
dedication, Baptists define child dedication as chiefly a
formal ceremony for publicly presenting a baby to God,
although the ceremony may also serve as an occasion for
both parents and congregation to acknowledge publicly
their responsibilities towards the child being dedicated.
Child dedication is different from the biblical ordinance
of baptism. Moreover, Baptists make it clear that child
dedication is not God's guarantee to parents that He will
save their child when he grows up.[10] But the main question
still remains: is there any scriptural evidence mandating a
child dedication service? Before answering this question,
an exploration of the historical origin of this practice will
first be given.

9. "Parent Child Dedication Services Planning Guide" (North Carolina:
Baptist State Convention of North Carolina, 2002), 5 (italics mine).

10. Aldrige, "The Parent-Child Dedication Service," 121–22.

STUDY QUESTIONS:

1. How do Baptists understand child dedication?

2. What is the difference between child dedication and infant baptism?

3. According to Baptists, can an infant become a member of a local church?

4. How do Baptists view their infants that have been dedicated to the Lord?

CHAPTER 2

TRACING THE HISTORICAL ORIGIN
OF CHILD DEDICATION

The practice of child dedication is commonly found among Baptist churches, although, as previously mentioned, not all Baptist churches practice it. The historical origin of child dedication in the Baptist tradition is obscure, yet traces of the practice begin to appear in the mid-seventeenth century in Britain. Outside Baptist circles, there is an identifiable lineage for the practice amidst Eastern Orthodox churches. Within this denomination, the process is called *forty-day churching*, or, as shortened, *churching*.

This ceremony, according to Greek Orthodox Ron Grove, is "a form of dedication of forty-day-old children that normally precedes baptism."[1] The Saint Barbara Greek Orthodox Church explains the ceremony:

> When the mother and child return from the hospital, it is traditional for them to observe a period of 40 days during which they rest and recuperate from the

---

1. Ron Grove, "Baby Dedication in Traditional Christianity: Eastern Orthodox 'Churching' of Forty-Day-Olds," *Journal of Ecumenical Studies* 27:1 (Winter 1990): 101.

delivery and refrain from travelling outside the home. The first place that the child is brought, then, is the Church, and what a beautiful sign of our dedication and hopes for the child than to offer him/her to the Lord! The roots of this tradition are found in the Old Testament (see Leviticus 12), but the reason that they are still practiced is founded in the example set by Christ through His own participation in the Temple (see Luke 2:22–40).[2]

As outlined by the quotation, the Greek Orthodox trace the roots of their churching service from the Old Testament, quoting Leviticus 12. Further, to defend their practice of it today, they advance Luke 2:22–40, which is also one of the passages that Baptists use to uphold their dedication service.

While churching is comparable with the Baptistic child dedication, sharp distinctions should be made between the two. Unlike Baptists, the Greek Orthodox hold a churching service to "church" the child, which is attested to represent "the entry of the child into the mystical body of Christ (although not into full membership), symbolized by its entrance into the physical temple."[3] Here, churching almost becomes a means of salvation.

---

2. Saint Barbara Greek Orthodox Church, Orange, CT, "40 Day Churching"; accessed 11 November 2011; available from http://saintbarbara .org/faith/sacraments/baptism/baptism.php; Internet.

3. Grove, "Baby Dedication in Traditional Christianity: Eastern Orthodox 'Churching' of Forty-Day-Olds," 102–103.

The Greek Orthodox also connect their churching to the Middle Ages.[4] They avow that "[t]he ritual of the 'churching' of women after childbirth has its origin in the early Middle Ages. This was the time when the liturgical life of the Church was beginning to expand and develop in imitation of the Biblical patterns."[5] However, as noted previously, unlike the Greek Orthodox, Baptists find it largely difficult to map the historical origin of their practice of child dedication.

Contesting this difficulty and offering a possible solution, Richard Leonard suggests that "[a]lthough its origins are obscure, the modern practice of dedicating children to God appears to have originated among Anglo-American revivalist Congregationalists and Baptists in the eighteenth century."[6] Similarly, R. L. Child attempts to document the development of child dedication in England during the latter half of the eighteenth century and into the nineteenth century. He "admits [also] that its origin is obscure."[7] Offering a

---

4. For a discussion of baby dedication in the patristic period, see David F. Wright, "Infant Dedication in the Early Church," in *Baptism, the New Testament and the Church: Historical and Contemporary Studies in Honour of R.E.O. White*, eds. Stanley E. Porter and Anthony R. Cross (Sheffield: Sheffield Academic Press, 1999), 352–78.

5. Annunciation Greek Orthodox Church, Modesto, CA, "Prayers for the New Born"; accessed 10 November 2011; available from http://www.forministry.com/USCAGOARCAGOCA/Orthodoxy.dsp; Internet.

6. Richard C. Leonard, "Child Dedication," in *The Sacred Actions of Christian Worship*, ed. Robert E. Webber (Nashville: Star Song Publishing Group, 1994), 267.

7. T. L. Underwood, "Child Dedication Services among British Baptists in the Seventeenth Century," *Baptist Quarterly* 23: 4 (October 1969): 165.

different view, T. L. Underwood suggests that the practice of child dedication existed as early as the mid-seventeenth century. In his brief article, "Child Dedication Services among British Baptists in the Seventeenth Century," Underwood demonstrates this view as conclusive. He contends that the practice emerged out of the desire of those who did not believe in infant baptism, even though they still had a desire to maintain a corresponding ceremony for their children.

To confirm his claim, Underwood cites Ralph Farmer (d. 1670) who wrote against those who practiced child dedication. Farmer, a staunch defender of infant baptism, denominated this practice as an "invention." In his *Sathan Inthron'd in his Chair of Pestilence* (1657), Farmer relates a story of a mother who refused to have her three children baptized. Relaying Farmer's story, Underwood writes that after speaking with one of her relatives, this mother realized "that although her children were surely in a better condition than the children of mere heathen, hers were like the children of heathen parents in not having been baptized." Underwood continues to survey, "The woman consulted the Teacher [i.e., Thomas Ewins (1617–1670)] of the church [of Independents and Baptists] about this problem and he in turn consulted the congregation. The result, according to Farmer, was that 'to give her satisfaction' the Teacher 'findes out this invention' [i.e., child dedication]."[8]

---

8. Underwood, "Child Dedication Services among British Baptists in the Seventeenth Century," 166–67. The story is recorded in Ralph Farmer's *Sathan Inthron'd in his Chair of Pestilence* (London: N.p, 1657). In this work,

The rebuttal of Thomas Ewins to Farmer's charge is worth mentioning here, found in *The Church of Christ in Bristol Recovering her Vail out of the hands of them that have smitten and wounded her, and taken it away* (1657). Underwood notes Ewins' disagreement:

> [He] denied Farmer's charge that the service was simply an "invention to give her satisfaction" and claimed that no one in the congregation considered the action to be in any way a form of baptism. Furthermore, he recommended such a service "to all sober Christians, especially such as are dissatisfied in their judgments and Consciences, about Infant Baptism,…" and cautioned such persons against being "too remiss in the duty of thankfulness, and too careless of the precious Souls of their Children, &c."[9]

This dedication service, Ewins declares, was also done by others in Wales.[10]

Farmer narrates the dedication service of these three children: "Their Church being solemnly convened, the three Children are brought into the presence, and something being prayed, and something spoken by one, and so by another (prayer before and after, is not much material:) The man (for I know not well what to call his Name of Office) having spoken against sprinkling of Infants, (being it may be the words of his institution to this new Ordinance) takes the Children, the one that was young into his arms; and the other two, who were able to go, by the hand; and having called them by their Names, present them to the Congregation." Cited in Underwood, "Child Dedication Services among British Baptists in the Seventeenth Century," 167.

9. Underwood, "Child Dedication Services among British Baptists in the Seventeenth Century," 168.

10. Arthur Patzia reports that "[i]n the 17th century the practice was quite common among the English General Baptists. The individual who is

The account above demonstrates that Baptistic child dedication was present in the seventeenth century and that it sprang from those who were unhappy with infant baptism but felt the need to present their babies to God. In reaction and as replacement, child dedication was offered for those who still felt the need to present their children to God. Thus, the rejection of infant baptism yielded fertile ground for child dedication to arise instead.

Writing about the situation in the eighteenth century, Leonard echoes a similar observation:

> Worshipers in churches practicing only believers' baptism may have desired a comparable rite of passage for their children, an act symbolic of the beginning of their spiritual pilgrimage as members of the church family. The result was a ceremony which carefully avoided the terminology of baptism, but accomplished the same end as a rite of initiation.[11]

In light of truths found in this quote, the paedobaptist R. Scott Clark asserts:

> Many Baptistic churches...allow the practice of baby dedication. It would appear that this rite substitutes for baptism of the children of believers. Why? Because

---

credited with popularizing the rite was a distinguished Baptist pastor and leader in England by the name of John Clifford (1836–1932). Although his services of dedication were held initially in the home, they were moved later to the church." Patzia, "Baby Dedication in the Believer's Church," *American Baptist Quarterly* 3:1 (March 1984): 65–66.

11. Leonard, "Child Dedication," 267–68.

believers instinctively know that they need to present their children to God. Like the altar call this is a human substitute for divinely instituted covenant signs and seals of baptism and the Lord's Supper. Baptism is the sign of entrance or initiation into the visible Covenant assembly (church). Baby dedication fulfills this function.[12]

Baptists, wishing to defend their practice of child dedication, rightly fall back to Scripture for support. They offer two texts to legitimize their observance of child dedication. But can Baptists really use these texts as warrant for this observance?

---

12. R. Scott Clark, "A Contemporary Reformed Defense of Infant Baptism"; accessed 11 November 2011; available from http://clark.wscal.edu/baptism.php; Internet. I owe this quote to Wayne Jackson, "Baby Dedication Ceremonies: Expediency or Innovation?": accessed 11 November 2011; available from http://www.christiancourier.com/articles/496-baby-dedication-ceremonies-expediency-or-innovation; Internet.

STUDY QUESTIONS:

1. Briefly trace the historical origin of child dedication.

2. How is Greek Orthodox forty-day churching comparable with Baptistic child dedication? What is the difference between the two?

3. What do you think of Ralph Farmer's observation that child dedication is an invention to satisfy parents who disagree with infant baptism?

4. Thomas Ewins advises parents who are dissatisfied in their consciences about infant baptism to practice child dedication. Do you think his recommendation is wise?

CHAPTER 3

EXAMINING CHILD DEDICATION IN LIGHT OF GOD'S WORD

There are two scriptural texts that are commonly used to justify the practice of child dedication: 1 Samuel 1:11, 22–24 and Luke 2:22–24. With reference to both of these passages, Baptists do not propose that either *explicitly commands* child dedication. However, Baptists claim that both passages *implicitly commend* child dedication.

Art Kohl, a Baptist pastor, pointedly agrees. He argues that child dedication is implicitly commended in Scripture. He writes, "It might be wise, but not necessary for a parent to 'officially' dedicate their child to the Lord in a public service. That is between the parents and God."[1] This should be carefully noted, as in a few Baptist churches today child dedication is unfortunately regarded as almost directly commanded. Parents are made to feel guilty if they do not dedicate their children to God. Certainly, in light of this

---

1. Art Kohl, "Baby Baptism or Baby Dedication: Which is Biblical?"; accessed 12 November 2011 available from http://www.fbbc.com/messages/baby_dedication.htm; Internet.

trepidation, careful examination of both 1 Samuel 1 and Luke 2 is required.

The Example of Hannah's Bringing Samuel to the House of the LORD

Advocates of child dedication support their practice with Hannah's example in 1 Samuel 1. Those who employ this example, however, reveal a lack of knowledge about the unique context of Hannah. First, Hannah had been infertile and had vowed to dedicate her child to the Lord if He would bless her. Thus, when she bore a child, Samuel, she brought him to God's house in fulfillment of her vow that if God gave her a son she would "give him to the LORD all the days of his life" (1 Sam. 1:11). Dissimilarly, parents today do not dedicate their child to fulfill a vow. Second, Hannah offered her son specifically as a Nazarite, as confirmed by the expression "no razor shall come upon his head" (1 Sam. 1:11). Third, she did not bring her child to God's house until her child could be weaned, probably at the age of three years old (1 Sam. 1:22). Normally Baptist parents dedicate their child before three years of age. Fourth, Hannah brought her son to be a priest in the temple, "that he [might] appear before the LORD and remain there forever" (1 Sam. 1:22). Certainly, when parents dedicate their child, it is not directly to the vocational service of the Lord. Parents are not expected to dedicate their child to be a minister. Fifth, Hannah offered her child "with three bulls, one ephah of flour, and a skin of wine" (1 Sam.

1:24). When parents dedicate their child today, they do not bring an offering of any kind. Finally, Hannah alone, it appears, made the decision to offer Samuel to the Lord, though Elkanah, her husband, does seem to at least give his blessing on her decision (1 Sam. 1:23). Further, it appears that Hannah also went alone to the temple to offer her son (1 Sam. 1:28). In contrast, when parents dedicate their child today, both decide and act together as a couple.

Does Hannah's example then support the modern practice of child dedication? From the strong contrasts above the answer is a resounding no! Hannah's case was unique and therefore should not be taken as a norm. In summary, child dedication cannot be commended by citing this passage, as the text reveals a special case of vow-fulfillment and does not equate to a general prescription of child dedication.

The Example of Mary and Joseph's Bringing Jesus to the Temple

Baptists refer to another passage to sanction their avowal of child dedication. They offer Luke 2:22–24 and suggest that the presentation of Jesus by His parents to the Lord equates to a commendation of child dedication. But can they use this text for support of this practice? A careful examination of this text will affirm another emphatic no.

In the first place, the presentation of Jesus in the temple should be understood in light of the law of purification in Leviticus 12. This passage is worth quoting here:

Then the LORD spoke to Moses, saying, "Speak to the children of Israel, saying: 'If a woman has conceived, and borne a male child, then she shall be unclean seven days…. And on the eighth day the flesh of his foreskin shall be circumcised. She shall then continue in the blood of *her* purification thirty-three days. She shall not touch any hallowed thing, nor come into the sanctuary until the days of her purification are fulfilled…'When the days of her purification are fulfilled, whether for a son or a daughter, she shall bring to the priest a lamb of the first year as a burnt offering, and a young pigeon or a turtledove as a sin offering, to the door of the tabernacle of meeting. Then he shall offer it before the LORD, and make atonement for her. And she shall be clean from the flow of her blood. This *is* the law for her who has borne a male or a female. And if she is not able to bring a lamb, then she may bring two turtledoves or two young pigeons—one as a burnt offering and the other as a sin offering. So the priest shall make atonement for her, and she will be clean.'"

Compare the above passage to Luke's record:

Now when the days of her purification according to the law of Moses were completed, they brought Him to Jerusalem to present *Him* to the Lord (as it is written in the law of the Lord, *"Every male who opens the womb shall be called holy to the LORD"*), and to offer a sacrifice according to what is said in the law of the Lord, *"A pair of turtledoves or two young pigeons."*

In the light of these passages, two important observations must be made. First, Mary and Joseph acted according to the ceremony of purification. It was in this context that they presented their child Jesus to the Lord in the temple. According to the Levitical law, Mary was considered unclean for forty days after the birth of Jesus. This means that Mary could not come into the temple to participate in any religious activities with the congregation until she was ceremonially purified (Lev. 12:4). When Jesus turned eight days old, He was circumcised according to the law (Gen. 17:12; Lev. 12:3; Luke 2:21). Thirty-three days later (i.e., when Jesus was forty days old) when the days of Mary's purification were finished, she and Joseph presented Jesus to the Lord.

This is in sharp contrast to the modern practice of child dedication, for it has nothing to do with the ceremonial law of purification. Indeed, parents today should realize that there is no need for them to observe any ceremonial law at all, as Christ fulfilled it entirely! Thus, there is no basis to be found for child dedication in Mary and Joseph's act. Luke does not emphasize the fact that Mary and Joseph presented the baby Jesus but the fact that Jesus submitted Himself to this law and fulfilled it (Matt. 5:17; Gal. 4:4).

In the second place, Mary and Joseph presented their son Jesus to the Lord within the framework of the Old Testament Passover. Luke records, "[T]hey brought Him to Jerusalem [where the temple was] to present *Him* to the Lord (as it is written in the law of the Lord, '*Every male who opens the womb shall be called holy to the LORD*')." The italicized sentence is a quote from Exodus 13:

> Then the LORD spoke to Moses, saying, "Consecrate to Me all the firstborn, whatever opens the womb among the children of Israel, *both* of man and beast; it is Mine".... "And it shall be, when the LORD brings you into the land of the Canaanites, as He swore to you and your fathers, and gives it to you, that you shall set apart to the LORD all that open the womb, that is, every firstborn that comes from an animal which you have; the males *shall be* the LORD's. But every firstborn of a donkey you shall redeem with a lamb; and if you will not redeem *it,* then you shall break its neck. And all the firstborn of man among your sons you shall redeem. So it shall be, when your son asks you in time to come, saying, 'What *is* this?' that you shall say to him, 'By strength of hand the LORD brought us out of Egypt, out of the house of bondage. And it came to pass, when Pharaoh was stubborn about letting us go, that the LORD killed all the firstborn in the land of Egypt, both the firstborn of man and the firstborn of beast. Therefore I sacrifice to the LORD all males that open the womb, but all the firstborn of my sons I redeem.' It shall be as a sign on your hand and as frontlets between your eyes, for by strength of hand the LORD brought us out of Egypt."

According to the law portrayed above, the baby Jesus, because He was a first-born son, was regarded as holy or set apart to the Lord. Thus, He was to be presented to God in the temple (Ex. 13:2). The presentation was done in remembrance of God's deliverance of the Israelites' first-born from death in Egypt through the sprinkling of the blood (Ex. 13:16). According to the law, Jesus, as a first-born son, was also to be redeemed by the offering of a sacrifice (Ex. 13:13–15; Num. 18:15). The Baptist commentator John Gill explains this well:

> The reason of this law was this, when God smote all the firstborn of Egypt, he saved the firstborn of Israel; and therefore claimed a right to them, and obliged their parents, excepting the Levites, to redeem them at the price of five shekels, which were about twelve shillings and six pence of our money, and which was given to the Levites.… And this law our Lord came under as Mary's firstborn, and as one holy to the Lord; and such a sum of money was now paid for his redemption, who was the great Redeemer of his people: he being made under the law, and in all things subject to it, that he might redeem them from the bondage, curse, and condemnation of it. Now as the tribe of Levi was excepted from this law, it is a clear case, that Mary, though allied to Elisabeth, was not of the tribe of Levi, otherwise her firstborn would not have been subject to it.[2]

Because this passage deals with fulfilling the law of Exodus, to use Luke 2:22–24 to support the modern practice of child dedication is a failure to understand the historical

---

2. John Gill, *Exposition of the Old and New Testament*, vol. 7 (London: Mathews and Leigh, 1809), 525.

context of the passage. Mary and Joseph presented Jesus in the temple in obedience to the Mosaic law. Their motivation did not stem from a desire to promise God that they would raise their child in the ways of the Lord.

One more passage deserves attention: Matthew 19:13–15, which is sometimes quoted during a child dedication service. It reads: "Then little children were brought to Him that He might put *His* hands on them and pray, but the disciples rebuked them. But Jesus said, 'Let the little children come to Me, and do not forbid them; for of such is the kingdom of heaven.' And He laid *His* hands on them and departed from there." Although this passage speaks about children, it has nothing to do with the modern rite of child dedication. Rather, the passage stresses that the kingdom of heaven is for those who have a child-like faith (Matt. 18:3). It does not relate to child dedication, and therefore it cannot be used to support the position.

With regards to the passages examined in this chapter, it appears that certainly none command the practice of child dedication. Further, as none of the passages deal with child dedication specifically, they cannot be used to commend the practice either. None of these passages provide scriptural warrant that exalts the practice.

STUDY QUESTIONS:

1. Is child dedication commanded in the Bible? If not, should churches observe it?

2. What is the main reason why Hannah's example cannot be used to support the modern practice of child dedication?

3. How must Luke 2:22–24 be interpreted in relation to child dedication?

4. What other passages are commonly cited to justify child dedication? Do you think these passages support this practice?

CONCLUSION

After examining the alleged biblical support for the practice of child dedication, a conclusion can be made that this kind of dedicatory service is not commanded in the Scriptures. Hence, parents should not feel guilty if they do not present their children to the Lord through this service. The Bible does not require them to have such a ceremony for their children. Child dedication is not a divinely ordained rite. According to Scripture, the Lord has instituted only two sacraments for His Church: baptism (Matt. 28:19–20) and the Lord's Supper (1 Cor. 11:23–26). The Heidelberg Catechism (1563) rightly explains:

> The sacraments are visible holy signs and seals appointed by God for this end, that by their use He may the more fully declare and seal to us the promise of the Gospel, namely, that of free grace He grants us the forgiveness of sins and everlasting life for the sake of the one sacrifice of Christ accomplished on the cross (Gen. 17:11; Rom. 4:11; Deut. 30:6; Heb. 9:8–9; Ezek. 20:12).[1]

1. *The Heidelberg Catechism* (1563) in *Reformed Confessions of the 16th*

Since child dedication is not a command, do parents sin if they observe it? I do not think so. It is comparable to dedicating a new seminary building: the practice is not necessary, nor mandated by Scripture, yet it can serve positively to bind the dedicators to honoring the Lord. We dedicate a newly acquired building in public (though it could be done in private) to acknowledge openly the fact that it is from the Lord, that we are only stewards of it, and therefore, that we are expected to take care of it. In like manner, so is it with child dedication. If we can dedicate a building to the Lord, can we not also dedicate a baby to Him? In fact, some paedobaptists will admit that there is nothing wrong for Christian parents to dedicate their children to the Lord. John Frame, a well-known paedobaptist theologian, says:

> My personal view is that dedicating children is a good thing to do. If we are to dedicate everything in our lives to Christ, then certainly we should dedicate our children. I don't know of any Scripture that says it has to be by a specific church ceremony (unless that ceremony is the sacrament of Baptism). But, like a wedding, I don't think Scripture prohibits it.[2]

---

and 17th Centuries in English Translation: Volume 2, 1552–1566, compiled with introductions by James T. Dennison, Jr. (Grand Rapids: Reformation Heritage Books, 2010), 784.

2. John Frame said this to me in our email conversation dated 5 November 2011.

I do propose that God expects parents to entrust their children to His care and raise them under His authority. In this manner, some Christian parents "dedicate" their children informally. Others choose to dedicate their children publicly with the congregation. As this booklet argues, this formal child dedication is certainly not required by Scripture, but I do not see a problem if parents practice it as long as the following two restrictions are maintained. First, parents must not make child dedication as a substitute for the ordinance of infant baptism. Second, parents must not view child dedication as a God-appointed element of the worship service. From these restrictions it quickly follows, that if child dedication is not ordained as an act of worship, then parents should not perform it during the worship service. The regulative principle of worship negates the possibility that child dedication occur during a worship service. I therefore pastorally advise that, should parents decide voluntarily to hold a dedicatory service for their child, they should not do it during the worship service. As dedicators wish to worship and honor God in their act of dedication, they can learn from what is written in the Westminster Confession of Faith (1646) regarding religious worship and the Sabbath Day:

> ...the acceptable way of worshipping the true God is instituted by Himself, and so limited by His own revealed will, that He may not be worshipped according to the imaginations and devices of men, or the suggestions of Satan, under any visible representation,

or any other way not prescribed in the holy Scripture (Deut. 12:32; Matt. 15:9; Acts 17:25; Matt. 4:9–10; Deut. 15:1–20; Ex. 20:4–6; Col. 2:23).[3]

Further, since the concept of dedication is embedded in the observance of the Reformed doctrine of infant baptism, paedobaptist parents do not need to consider the celebration of child dedication. When we, paedobaptist parents, baptize our children in the name of the triune God, we also dedicate them to God. We promise at their baptism to raise our children in the fear of the Lord. In fact, during the administration of baptism, we use the following liturgical form in which parents are asked to promise to bring up their child in the nurture and admonition of the Lord:

The minister addresses the parents:

Since you have presented this child…for holy baptism, you are asked to answer the following questions before God and his people:

First, do you confess Jesus Christ as your Lord and Savior, accept the promises of God, and affirm the truth of the Christian faith which is proclaimed in the Bible and confessed in this church of Christ?

Second, do you believe that your child, though sinful by nature, is received by God in Christ as a member of his covenant, and therefore ought to be baptized?

---

3. *The Westminster Confession of Faith* (1646), in *Reformed Confessions of the 16th and 17th Centuries in English Translation: Volume 4, 1600–1693*, compiled with introductions by James T. Dennison, Jr. (Grand Rapids: Reformation Heritage Books, 2014), 258.

Third, do you promise, in reliance on the Holy Spirit and with the help of the Christian community, to do all in your power to instruct this child in the Christian faith and to lead him by your example into the life of Christian discipleship?

The parents respond: We do, God helping us.

The minister addresses the congregation:

Do you, the people of the Lord, promise to receive this child in love, pray for him, help care for his instruction in the faith, and encourage and sustain him in the fellowship of believers?

The congregation responds: We do, God helping us.[4]

In conclusion, I think infant dedication was born out of the natural Christian instinct of parents who did not agree with the biblical doctrine of infant baptism but desired to have a corresponding rite for their children. Arthur Patzia has a commendable point, and I agree heartily:

[T]he rise and popularity of baby dedication coincided with the emergence of the Sunday School movement with its emphasis upon the Christian nurture of children rather than with some biblical or theological conviction. The personal gratitude for the birth of a child and the parental commitment to

---

4. See Liturgical Form for Baptism of Children in *Psalter Hymnal* (1976), 130–31.

provide a Christian home was transferred to the context of the church.[5]

I hope that this study will also encourage those who practice child dedication to consider the Reformed doctrine of infant baptism.

5. Arthur Patzia, "Baby Dedication in the Believer's Church," *American Baptist Quarterly* 3:1 (March 1984): 66.

BIBLIOGRAPHY

Aldrige, Marion D. "The Parent-Child Dedication Service," in *The Pastors' Guide Book: A Manual for Worship*. Nashville: Broadman Press, 1984, 121–31.

Annunciation Greek Orthodox Church, Modesto, CA, "Prayers for the New Born." Accessed 10 November 2011. Available from http://www.forministry.com/USCAGOARCAGOCA/Orthodoxy.dsp; Internet.

Barcellos, Richard. *Baby Dedications Ancient and Modern: Are They Biblical?* Fullerton: Reformed Baptist Publication, n. d.

Clark, R. Scott. "A Contemporary Reformed Defense of Infant Baptism." Accessed 11 November 2011. Available from http://clark.wscal.edu/baptism.php; Internet.

De Moor, Henry. "Erosion at the Font," *Calvin Theological Journal* 29:1 (April 1994): 168–79.

Farmer, Ralph. *Sathan Inthron'd in his Chair of Pestilence*. London: N.p, 1657.

Frame, John. Email conversation. Dated 5 November 2011.

Gill, John. *Exposition of the Old and New Testament*. Vol. 7. London: Mathews and Leigh, 1809.

Grove, Ron "Baby Dedication in Traditional Christianity: Eastern Orthodox 'Churching' of Forty-Day-Olds," *Journal of Ecumenical Studies* 27:1 (Winter 1990): 101–107.

Hyde, Daniel R. *Jesus Loves the Little Children: Why We Baptize Children*. Grandville: Reformed Fellowship, Inc., 2006.

Jackson, Wayne. "Baby Dedication Ceremonies: Expediency or Innovation?." Accessed 11 November 2011. Available from http://www.christiancourier.com/articles/496-baby-dedication-ceremonies-expediency-or-innovation; Internet.

Kohl, Art. "Baby Baptism or Baby Dedication: Which is Biblical?" Accessed 12 November 2011. Available from http://www.fbbc.com/messages/baby_dedication.htm; Internet.

Leonard, Richard C. "Child Dedication," in *The Sacred Actions of Christian Worship*. Edited by Robert E. Webber. Nashville: Star Song Publishing Group, 1994, 267–71.

Neighborhood Church of Castro Valley, CA, "Infant Dedication Services." Accessed 9 November 2011. Available from http://www.3crosses.org/neighborhood/pages/7-infant-dedication-services; Internet.

"Parent Child Dedication Services Planning Guide." North Carolina: Baptist State Convention of North Carolina, 2002.

Patzia, Arthur. "Baby Dedication in the Believer's Church," *American Baptist Quarterly* 3:1 (March 1984): 63–72.

Psalter Hymnal (1976).

Saint Barbara Greek Orthodox Church, Orange, CT, "40 Day Churching." Accessed 11 November 2011. Available from http://saintbarbara.org/faith/sacraments/baptism/baptism.php; Internet.

Siler, M. Mahan. "Rites of Passage: A Meeting of Worship and Pastoral Care," *Review and Expositor* 85 (1988): 51–61.

The Heidelberg Catechism (1563).

The Westminster Confession of Faith (1646).

Underwood, T. L. "Child Dedication Services among British Baptists in the Seventeenth Century," *Baptist Quarterly* 23: 4 (October 1969): 165–69.

Wright, David F. "Infant Dedication in the Early Church," in *Baptism, the New Testament and the Church: Historical and Contemporary Studies in Honour of R.E.O. White*. Edited by Stanley E. Porter and Anthony R. Cross. Sheffield: Sheffield Academic Press, 1999, 352–78.

ABOUT THE AUTHOR

 Born and reared in the Philippines, Brian G. Najapfour has been a minister of God since 2001. Called to the gospel ministry at the young age of sixteen, he began his theological education in 1997 at the Center for Biblical Studies Institute and Seminary in the Philippines. There, with God's help, he earned his Bachelor of Theology (B.Th.) degree in 2001, followed by his Master in Biblical Studies (M.B.S.) degree in 2004. From 2001 until his coming to the U.S. in 2006, he served as a pastor in the Philippines. With a desire to further his education, however, he arrived in Grand Rapids, Michigan in 2006, where he enrolled in Puritan Reformed Theological Seminary. There, he studied for his Master of Theology (Th.M.) degree, which he completed by God's grace in 2009.

While pursuing a Ph.D. degree, Najapfour, since his installation on October 19, 2012, has been pastor of Dutton United Reformed Church in Caledonia, Michigan. He is co-editor (along with Joel R. Beeke) of *Taking Hold of God: Reformed and Puritan Perspectives on Prayer* (2011) and author of *The Very Heart of Prayer: Reclaiming John Bunyan's Spirituality* (2012) and *Jonathan Edwards: His Doctrine of and Devotion to Prayer* (2013).

For more information about him, visit his website:
biblicalspiritualitypress.org